The Compound Effect of Habits

How to Build Lasting Habits for Personal and Professional Growth

THE COMPOUND EFFECT OF

HABITS

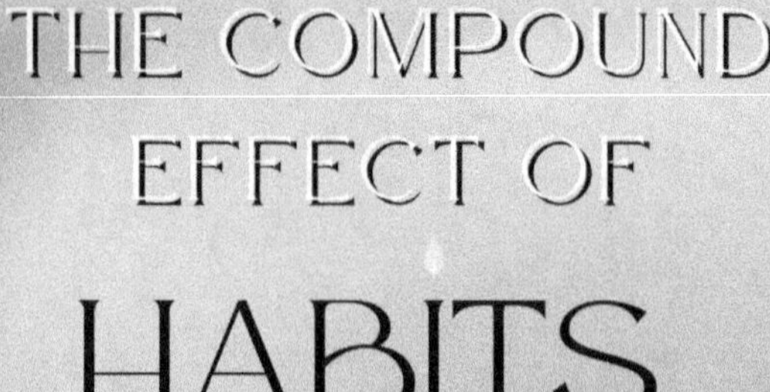

How to Build Lasting Habits for Personal and Professional Growth

MARTIN RINCON

Table of Contents

Introduction

Welcome to "The Compound Effect of Habits: How to Build Lasting Habits for Personal and Professional Growth"! This book will explore the power of small, consistent choices and how they can lead to significant and lasting change in our lives.

Have you ever heard the saying, "The sum of small efforts, repeated day in and day out, leads to the successful person"? This is the essence of the compound effect, and it's a concept that can also be applied to our habits. Every action we take, no matter how small, impacts our lives. When we consistently make good choices, they lead to positive change. But, on the other hand, when we consistently make poor choices, they can hold us back from reaching our goals and living our best lives.

So, how can we harness the power of the compound effect to build lasting habits that help us achieve personal and professional growth? That's what we will be exploring in this book. We'll delve into the science behind habits and how they are formed and practical strategies for building good habits and breaking bad ones. We'll also explore the role of mindset in habit formation and how to overcome common obstacles like procrastination and lack of motivation.

In addition to providing practical tips and exercises, this book will also be filled with You'll see how small, consistent choices have led to significant and lasting changes in health, relationships, finances, productivity, and more.

Whether you're looking to make a small change or a complete overhaul, this book will provide the tools and strategies you need to build lasting habits and create the life you want. So, let's get started on this journey toward personal and professional growth!

Chapter I. The Power of Small Choices

We often underestimate the power of small choices. One cookie won't make a difference in our health, or skipping one day of exercise won't impact our fitness goals. We tell ourselves that it's just one small choice, and it won't matter in the grand scheme of things.

But the truth is small choices have a cumulative effect. They may seem insignificant at the moment, but when we consistently make good or bad choices, they compound and significantly impact our lives. This is the essence of the compound effect, and it's a concept that can also be applied to our habits. That is also why I choose the title for this book.

Think about it this way: if you eat one cookie today, it will not significantly impact your health. But if you eat one cookie every day for a month, that's an additional 30 cookies in your diet. Over time, those small choices add up and can significantly impact your health and wellness goals. The same is true for exercise. Skipping one day of exercise may not seem like a big deal, but if you consistently skip your workouts, it can significantly hold you back from reaching your fitness goals.

The good news is the compound effect works in our favor as well. When we consistently make good choices, they compound and lead to positive change. For example, if you always eat a healthy diet and exercise regularly, those choices will compound and lead to improved health and wellness.

The power of small choices is not limited to health and fitness. It can be applied to any area of our lives, including relationships, finances, productivity, and personal growth. When we consistently make good choices in these areas, they compound and lead to positive changes and improvements.

So, how can we harness the power of small choices to build lasting habits and create the life we want? The key is to be mindful of our favorites and ensure they align with our values and goals. Every action we take, no matter how small, impacts our lives. By making conscious, deliberate choices, we can use the compound effect to our advantage and create the life we want.

It's important to remember that building lasting habits takes time and effort. It's not about making one big change, but rather making consistent, small choices over time. As the saying goes, "The sum of small efforts, repeated day in and day out, leads to the successful person." So take into account the power of small choices. They may seem insignificant at the moment, but they can have a significant and lasting impact on your life.

Chapter II. Understanding the Compound Effect

The compound effect is the idea that small, consistent choices lead to significant and lasting change over time. It's a simple concept that needs to be noticed and considered. We often focus on the big, dramatic changes we want to make, but the small, consistent choices we make daily have the biggest impact on our lives.

To better understand the compound effect, let's look at an example. Imagine you have a goal to save $10,000 in the next year. You could achieve this goal by making one big, drastic change, like quitting your job and starting a new business. While this might seem like a bold and exciting move, it's also risky and may fail to guarantee success. On the other hand, you could achieve the same goal by making small, consistent choices that add up over time. For example, you could save $100 a month by cutting back on unnecessary expenses and investing the extra money in a high-yield savings account. Over the course of a year, these small, consistent choices would add up to $1,200 in savings, which is a significant contribution towards your $10,000 goal.

The compound effect works in the same way for building habits. When we consistently make good choices, they compound and lead to positive change. For example, if you have a habit of exercising for 30 minutes a day, that's a small, consistent choice that will positively impact your health and wellness. But if you consistently skip your workouts, that's a small, consistent choice that will keep you from reaching your fitness goals.

So, how can we use the compound effect to our advantage? The key is to focus on small, consistent choices that align with our values and goals. This might mean reducing unhealthy habits like smoking or excessive drinking or making minor changes to your diet and exercise routine. It could also mean making small, consistent personal or professional development investments, like taking a course or networking with others in your field.

It's important to remember that the compound effect takes time to work. It's not about making one significant, dramatic change but rather making small, consistent choices over time. It's also important to be patient and persistent. Building lasting habits takes time and effort, but the compound effect will work in your favor as long as you stay consistent and committed.

In summary, the compound effect is the idea that small, consistent choices lead to significant and lasting change over time. By focusing on small, consistent choices that align with our values and goals, we can harness the power of the compound effect to create the life we want. Remember to be patient and persistent, as lasting building habits takes time and effort. But with consistent and committed action, the compound effect will work in your favor and help you achieve your goals and live your best life.

Chapter III. Setting Habitable Goals

Goal setting is vital for building lasting habits and creating the life you want. But not all goals are created equal. To be effective, goals should be "habitable," meaning they are achievable, specific, and aligned with your values and priorities.

One common mistake people make when setting goals is setting goals that should be narrower and more specific. For example, a goal like "lose weight" or "save more money" is too broad and not specific enough. It's essential to be specific and quantify your goals so you have a clear target to work towards. For example, a specific and quantifiable goal might be "lose 10 pounds in the next three months" or "save $500 per month for the next year." Specific, measurable goals are more achievable and provide a clear target.

Another critical aspect of habitable goals is that they should be aligned with your values and priorities. Your goals should be things that are important to you and that you are motivated to work towards. If your goals are not aligned with your values and priorities, it's easy to lose motivation and give up.

So, how can you set habitable goals? Here are a few tips:

- Start with your values and priorities. What are the most important things to you? What do you want to achieve in your life?
- Make your goals specific and quantifiable. For example, instead of setting a broad goal like "lose weight," set a specific purpose like "lose 10 pounds in the next three months."
- Make your goals achievable. Set realistic goals that you can work towards without becoming overwhelmed or discouraged.

- Break your goals down into smaller, more manageable tasks. This will make your goals more achievable and give you a sense of progress as you work towards them.
- Write your goals down and plan. A written plan helps keep you accountable and motivated as you work towards your goals.

By setting wearable goals, you'll be more likely to stay motivated and committed as you work towards building lasting habits. Remember to be patient and persistent, as building lasting habits takes time and effort. But with clear, wearable goals and a plan to achieve them, you'll be on your way to creating the life you want.

Chapter IV. Creating a Supportive Environment

When it comes to building lasting habits, our environment plays a crucial role. Our surroundings can either support or hinder our efforts to make positive changes in our lives. Therefore, creating an environment that promotes the habits we want to build is crucial.

There are several ways to create a supportive environment for habit formation:

1. Surround yourself with supportive people. The people we surround ourselves with significantly impact our habits and behavior. We are more likely to succeed if we surround ourselves with people who support and encourage our goals. On the other hand, if we surround ourselves with people who are negative or unsupportive, it can be harder to stick to our habits and make positive changes. So, it's essential to surround ourselves with people who will support and encourage us as we work towards building lasting habits.

2. Remove distractions and temptations. Our environment can be full of distractions and temptations that hinder our efforts to build lasting habits. For example, if you are trying to develop a habit of exercising regularly but have a TV in your exercise room, watching TV instead of working out can be tempting. Similarly, if you are trying to build a habit of eating a healthy diet, but you have unhealthy snacks in your pantry, it can be tempting to indulge in those instead of sticking to your healthy habits. By removing distractions and temptations from our environment, we can make it easier to stick to our habits and make positive changes.

3. Set up reminders and cues. Finally, our environment can also remind us to practice our habits. For example, suppose you are trying to build a habit of meditating daily. In that case, you could set up a reminder on your phone or place a meditation cushion in a visible location to remind you to

practice. Similarly, if you are trying to build a habit of flossing your teeth before bed, you could place a container of floss next to your toothbrush as a cue to remember to floss.

4. Establish routines and rituals. Establishing routines and rituals can make our habits feel more automatic and effortless. For example, if you are trying to exercise regularly, you could set a morning routine that includes a walk or yoga practice. Making your habit part of a daily routine or ritual can become more ingrained and easier to stick to.

5. Make your environment visually appealing. Our environment can also have an impact on our mood and motivation. By making our environment visually appealing, we can create a sense of positivity and encouragement that can support our habits. For example, you could add plants, artwork, or other decorative elements to your environment to make it feel more welcoming and uplifting.

By creating a supportive environment, we can set ourselves up for success as we work towards building lasting habits. Remember that it takes time and effort to build lasting habits, but with a supportive environment and the right mindset, it's possible to create the life you want.

Chapter V. Breaking Bad Habits

We all have habits that hold us back from living our best lives. These bad habits can range from unhealthy behaviors like smoking or overeating to unproductive habits like procrastination or negative thinking. Whatever the bad habit, it's essential to recognize and address it to make positive changes in our lives.

So, how can we break bad habits and replace them with good ones? Here are a few strategies to try:

1. Identify the root cause of the habit. Before breaking a bad habit, it's essential to understand what's driving it. Is it boredom? Stress? A lack of motivation? By identifying the root cause of the habit, you can address the underlying issue and make it easier to break the habit.
2. Set a clear goal and plan. Once you understand the root cause of the habit, set a clear purpose for breaking the pattern and project how you will achieve it. For example, suppose you are trying to break the habit of procrastination. In that case, your goal might be to complete tasks as soon as they are assigned, and your plan might involve setting aside dedicated time for work, breaking large tasks into smaller chunks, and removing distractions.
3. Build supportive structures. Your environment can either support or hinder your efforts to break bad habits. By building supportive structures, you can make it easier to break bad habits and replace them with good ones. For example, if you break the habit of unhealthy eating, you might remove unhealthy snacks from your pantry and stock your fridge with healthy options instead.
4. Use rewards and incentives. Sometimes, it can be helpful to use rewards and incentives to motivate yourself to break bad habits. For example, if you are trying to break the smoking habit, you might reward yourself with something

you enjoy, like a massage or a new book, every week you go without smoking.

5. Track your progress. Tracking your progress can help you to stay motivated and committed to breaking your bad habits. For example, you could use a journal or a habit tracker app to record your progress and celebrate your small wins along the way.

6. Practice mindfulness. Mindfulness can be a helpful tool for breaking bad habits. By bringing awareness to your thoughts and actions, you can become more aware of your habits and make changes to them. For example, suppose you are trying to break the habit of negative thinking. In that case, you might practice mindfulness techniques like meditation or journaling to bring awareness to your negative thoughts and reframe them more positively.

7. Seek professional help. If you are struggling to break a bad habit impacting your quality of life, seek professional help. A therapist or coach can provide you with the support and guidance you need to break your bad habits and make lasting changes.

Chapter VI. Building Good Habits

Good habits are the foundation for a happy, healthy, and productive life. They can help us to achieve our goals, improve our relationships, and live our best lives. But building good habits can be challenging. It takes time, effort, and consistency. So, how can we create good habits and make them stick? Here are a few strategies to try:

1. Start small. Building good habits is about making small, consistent choices over time. So it's essential to start small and focus on one habit at a time. By starting small, you'll be more likely to stay motivated and committed to your habit, and you'll also be more likely to make it a lasting part of your life.
2. Make your habits specific and quantifiable. It's essential to be specific and quantify your habits, so you have a clear target to work towards. For example, instead of setting a broad goal like "exercise more," set a specific goal like "exercise for 30 minutes a day." Specific, quantifiable habits are more achievable and provide a clear target to work towards.
3. Identify your triggers and habits. Understanding the triggers that precede your habits can help you build better ones. For example, if you have a habit of snacking on unhealthy foods when you're stressed, you might identify stress as a trigger for that habit. By specifying your triggers and habits, you can plan for how to interrupt that pattern and build a new habit in its place.
4. Build new habits on top of existing ones. Building new habits is easier when they are connected to existing ones. For example, if you already have a habit of brushing your teeth in the morning, you could add a habit of flossing to your morning routine.
5. Make your habits rewarding. By linking your habits to something you enjoy, you'll be more likely to stick with

them. For example, if you are trying to exercise regularly, choose a form of exercise that you enjoy, like dancing or hiking, to make it more rewarding.

6. Use reminders and cues. Your environment can remind you and cue you to practice your habits.

7. Seek accountability. Having someone to hold you accountable can be a helpful tool for building good habits. For example, you could enlist the help of a friend, family member, or coach to hold you accountable and keep you on track.

8. Be patient and persistent. Building good habits takes time and effort. So, it's essential to be patient and persistent, as it can take several weeks or even months to turn a new habit into a lasting one. Remember to celebrate your small wins along the way, and don't get discouraged if you encounter setbacks.

By following these strategies, you can build good habits and make them stick. Of course, building good habits is a journey, and it takes time and effort to make them a lasting part of your life. But with patience, persistence, and the right mindset, you can create the life you want by building good habits.

Chapter VII. The Role of Consistency in Habit Formation

Consistency is a crucial component of habit formation. When we are consistent in our actions, turning those actions into lasting habits becomes more manageable. But consistency can be challenging to achieve, especially when it comes to building new habits. So, how can we be more consistent in our habits and make them stick?

Here are a few tips to try:

1. Make your habits a priority. To be consistent, we need to make our habits a priority. This means setting aside dedicated time and energy to practice our habits and making them a non-negotiable part of our daily routine.
2. Set achievable goals. Consistency is easier to achieve when we set achievable goals. By setting realistic goals that we can work towards without becoming overwhelmed or discouraged, we are more likely to stay consistent and make progress.
3. Be flexible. While consistency is important, it's also important to be flexible and adaptable. If we are too rigid in our habits, it can be easy to become discouraged and give up. We can find a balance between consistency and adaptability by being open to adjusting and trying new approaches.
4. Stay motivated. Consistency is easier to achieve when we are motivated and committed to our habits. Find ways to stay motivated and keep yourself accountable, whether through rewards, accountability partners, or tracking your progress.
5. Practice self-compassion. Building habits is a journey, and we must be kind to ourselves. If we encounter setbacks or struggles, it's important to practice self-compassion and recognize that building habits take time and effort.

By being consistent in our habits, we can make them a lasting part of our lives. Of course, building lasting habits takes time and effort, but with the right mindset and strategies, it's possible to achieve consistency and turn our actions into habits.

Chapter VIII. Tracking and Celebrating Progress

Tracking and celebrating progress is an essential aspect of building lasting habits. When we follow our progress, we can see how far we've come and stay motivated to continue. And when we celebrate our progress, it helps to reinforce our habits and make them feel more rewarding.

So, how can we track and celebrate progress in our habits? Here are a few ideas to try:

- Use a habit tracker. Habit trackers are a valuable tool for tracking and celebrating progress. You can use a habit tracker app, a journal, or even a simple checkmark system to record your progress. By tracking your progress, you can see how far you've come and stay motivated to continue.
- Celebrate small wins. It's important to celebrate your progress, no matter how small. Recognizing and celebrating small victories can reinforce your habits and make them feel more rewarding. This helps keep you motivated and committed to your habits.
- Reflect on your progress. Reflecting on your progress can help you gain insight into what's working and not. By reflecting on your progress, you can identify areas for improvement and adjust your habits as needed.
- Share your progress with others. Sharing your progress with others can provide accountability and support as you work towards your goals. For example, you might share your progress with a friend or family member or even on social media. You can get feedback, encouragement, and support as you work towards your goals by sharing your progress.

Tracking and celebrating progress is an essential aspect of building lasting habits. Using tools like habit trackers and celebrating your small wins, you can stay motivated and committed to your habits and make them an ongoing part of your life.

Chapter XIX. The Role of Mindset in Habits

The role of mindset in habits is critical to personal and professional growth. Your mindset can either support or hinder the formation and maintenance of healthy habits. For example, a fixed mindset, characterized by the belief that your abilities and characteristics are fixed and cannot be changed, can prevent you from trying new things or taking on challenges that may require the development of new habits. On the other hand, a growth mindset, characterized by the belief that your abilities and characteristics can be developed through effort and learning, can support the formation and maintenance of healthy habits.

One fundamental way in which mindset impacts habits is through motivation. Motivation is the driving force behind behavior and is influenced by your thoughts, feelings, and beliefs. For example, if you have a fixed mindset, you may be less motivated to try new things or take on challenges because you believe that your abilities are fixed and need to be improved. This can lead to a lack of effort and a failure to develop new habits. On the other hand, if you have a growth mindset, you are more motivated to try new things and take on challenges because your abilities can be developed through effort and learning. This can lead to more significant steps and a higher likelihood of developing new habits.

Another way in which mindset impacts habits is through resilience. Resilience is the ability to bounce back from setbacks and failures and is influenced by your mindset. For example, if you have a fixed mindset, you may view failures as a reflection of your inherent abilities and give up easily when faced with challenges. On the other hand, if you have a growth mindset, you may view failures as opportunities to learn and grow and be more resilient in the face of challenges. This resilience can help you to persist in the face of setbacks and continue working towards the development of new habits.

Mindset also plays a role in the way that you approach challenges and problem-solve. For example, if you have a fixed mindset, you may be less likely to seek out new challenges or try new approaches to problem-solving because you believe that your abilities are fixed and cannot be improved. On the other hand, if you have a growth mindset, you may be more open to trying new things and seeking out challenges because your abilities can be developed through effort and learning. This openness to new experiences and challenges can support the development of new habits.

In addition to motivation, resilience, and approach to challenges, mindset also impacts your overall attitude and outlook on life. A fixed mindset can lead to a defeatist attitude, while a growth mindset can lead to a positive and proactive attitude. A positive and proactive attitude can make adopting and maintaining healthy habits easier because you are more likely to see the benefits of the habits and be motivated to continue them.

So, how can you cultivate a growth mindset to support the development and maintenance of healthy habits? One way is to focus on learning and growth rather than outcomes and performance. This means setting challenging but achievable goals and viewing failures as opportunities to learn and grow, rather than as reflections of your inherent abilities. It also means being open to feedback and looking for ways to improve rather than seeing criticism as a personal attack.

Another way to cultivate a growth mindset is to surround yourself with people with a growth mindset. This includes seeking out mentors and role models who are committed to learning and growth and surrounding yourself with supportive friends and colleagues who encourage a growth mindset.

Finally, practicing mindfulness can also help to cultivate a growth mindset. Mindfulness is the practice of bringing your attention to the present moment without judgment. By focusing on the present moment, you can become more aware of your thoughts and beliefs and identify any fixed mindset beliefs that may be holding you back. You can then work to replace those fixed mindset beliefs with more growth-oriented beliefs.

In conclusion, the role of mindset in habits is crucial for personal and professional growth. A fixed mindset can hinder the formation and maintenance of healthy habits, while a growth mindset can support them. By cultivating a growth mindset, you can be more motivated, resilient, open to new challenges, and have a positive attitude, all of which can support healthy habits. This includes focusing on learning and growth, seeking out mentors and role models with a growth mindset, and practicing mindfulness. Adopting a growth mindset can create the foundation for lasting habits that will support your personal and professional growth.

Chapter X. Overcoming Procrastination

Procrastination is a common challenge that can hinder the formation and maintenance of healthy habits. It is defined as delaying or postponing tasks or activities, and various factors, including lack of motivation, focus, and clarity about the task at hand, can cause it. Overcoming procrastination requires understanding the underlying causes of procrastination and taking steps to address them.

One common cause of procrastination is a need for more motivation. When you are not motivated to complete a task, getting started and maintaining momentum can be difficult. To overcome this type of procrastination, it can be helpful to identify the reasons why you are not motivated and find ways to increase your motivation. This may include setting goals that are meaningful and relevant to you, breaking tasks down into smaller, more manageable chunks, and finding ways to make the tasks more enjoyable or rewarding. It is also helpful to enlist the help of a coach or mentor who can provide guidance and support as you work to increase your motivation.

Another cause of procrastination is a need for more focus. When you cannot focus on the task, making progress and completing the job promptly can be challenging. To overcome this type of procrastination, it can be helpful to eliminate distractions and create a conducive environment for productivity. This may include finding a quiet workspace, turning off notifications on your phone or computer, and setting aside dedicated blocks of time to work on tasks without interruptions. It is also helpful to practice mindfulness, which involves bringing your attention to the present moment without judgment, as this helps to increase focus and concentration.

More clarity about the task at hand can also contribute to procrastination. When you are unsure of what is expected of you or how to proceed, it can be challenging to start and make progress. To overcome this type of procrastination, clarifying the task and setting specific, measurable goals can be helpful. This may involve breaking the task into smaller, more manageable steps and creating a plan. It is also beneficial to seek feedback or guidance from a mentor or colleague to ensure that you are on the right track.

In addition to addressing the underlying causes of procrastination, there are several strategies you can use to overcome procrastination and build lasting habits. One approach is the Pomodoro Technique, which involves working in focused, 25-minute blocks with short breaks in between. This technique can help increase focus and productivity and can be a helpful way to get started on tasks you are feeling overwhelmed by. Another strategy is to use accountability to help motivate yourself to act. This may involve setting deadlines for yourself or enlisting the help of a coach or accountability partner to help you stay on track.

Finally, it can be helpful to cultivate a growth mindset, which involves the belief that your abilities and characteristics can be developed through effort and learning. A growth mindset can help you view challenges and setbacks as opportunities to learn and grow rather than failures. It can increase your motivation and resilience as you overcome procrastination and build lasting habits.

In conclusion, overcoming procrastination is essential in building lasting habits for personal and professional growth. It involves understanding the underlying causes of procrastination and taking steps to address them, using strategies such as the Pomodoro Technique and accountability to help increase focus and productivity, and cultivating a growth mindset to increase motivation and resilience. By overcoming procrastination, you can create the foundation for lasting habits that will support your personal and professional growth.

Chapter XI. The Habit of Planning and Prioritizing

The habit of planning and prioritizing is a critical aspect of personal and professional success. It involves setting goals, creating a roadmap for achieving them, and prioritizing tasks and activities based on their importance and impact. By developing this habit, you can increase your productivity, reduce stress, and achieve your goals more efficiently.

As we stated before, one key aspect of planning and prioritizing is setting clear and specific goals. Goals provide a sense of direction and purpose and help to focus your efforts on what is most important. When setting goals, it is important to make them SMART: Specific, Measurable, Achievable, Relevant, and Time-bound. Specific and clear goals provide a clear understanding of what you want to achieve. Measurable goals have quantifiable outcomes, so you can track your progress and know when you have achieved them. Achievable goals are realistic and within your reach, given your resources and constraints. Relevant goals are aligned with your values and priorities and contribute to your overall sense of purpose. Finally, time-bound goals have a specific deadline, which helps to create a sense of urgency and motivates you to act.

Once you have set clear and specific goals, the next step in the habit of planning and prioritizing is to create a roadmap for achieving those goals. This involves breaking your goals into smaller, more manageable tasks and activities and creating a plan for completing them. This may include creating a to-do list, scheduling tasks in your calendar, and creating deadlines for each task. It is important to be realistic and flexible in your planning, as unexpected challenges and changes will inevitably arise.

After you have set goals and created a roadmap for achieving them, the next step in the habit of planning and prioritizing is to prioritize tasks and activities based on their importance and impact. This involves evaluating each job with your goals and determining which jobs are most important and will impact your progress. You can use various tools and techniques to help you prioritize tasks. For example, the Eisenhower Matrix divides tasks into four categories: urgent and important, important but not urgent, urgent but not important, and not important or urgent. This can help you to identify which tasks are most critical and should be given priority.

In addition to setting goals, creating a roadmap, and prioritizing tasks, there are several other strategies we mentioned before that you could use to support the habit of planning and prioritizing. One approach is to use time management techniques, such as the Pomodoro Technique or the Time Blocking method, to help you focus on tasks and increase productivity. Another strategy is eliminating distractions and creating a conducive environment for productivity, such as finding a quiet workspace, turning off notifications on your phone or computer, and setting aside dedicated time to work on tasks without interruptions.

One important thing to remember is that developing the habit of planning and prioritizing takes time and effort. It may not come naturally initially, and you may encounter setbacks and challenges. However, with practice and persistence, you can build this habit and see the benefits in your personal and professional life. It may be helpful to enlist the help of a coach or mentor to provide guidance and support as you work to develop this habit.

Finally, it is essential to be flexible and adaptable in your planning and prioritizing. Unexpected challenges and changes will inevitably arise, and it is important to be willing to adjust your plan as needed in order to stay on track. This may involve modifying your goals, prioritizing tasks differently, or seeking support from others.

In conclusion, the habit of planning and prioritizing is a critical aspect of personal and professional success. It involves setting clear and specific goals, creating a roadmap for achieving those goals, and prioritizing tasks and activities based on their importance and impact. By developing this habit, you can increase productivity, reduce stress, and achieve your goals more efficiently. In addition to setting goals, creating a roadmap, and prioritizing tasks, several other strategies you can use to support the habit of planning and prioritizing, including using time management techniques, eliminating distractions, and being flexible and adaptable in your planning. By committing to planning and prioritizing, you can create the foundation for lasting habits that will support your personal and professional growth.

Chapter XII. The Habit of Time Planning

Effective time management is a critical skill that can greatly impact an individual's personal and professional life. It allows you to prioritize tasks, makes the most of your time, and ultimately achieve your goals. However, developing the habit of time management can be challenging. It requires discipline, focus, and a willingness to evaluate and adjust your habits continuously.

Creating a daily schedule is one way to start building time management habits. This can be as simple as jotting down a list of tasks you need to accomplish each day or more detailed, with specific blocks of time allocated for each activity. Having a schedule helps you stay organized and focused, and it can also help you identify areas where you may be wasting time.

Another important aspect of time management is setting goals, which means identifying what you want to accomplish, setting deadlines, and breaking down large goals into smaller, more manageable tasks. You can track your progress and adjust your schedule as needed by setting clear goals.

One common obstacle to effective time management is the tendency to multitask. While it may seem like multitasking allows you to get more done in a shorter amount of time, it can be counterproductive. When you multitask, you split your attention and often need to give each task the full focus it requires. This can lead to mistakes and inefficiencies and can also be mentally exhausting. Instead of multitasking, try to focus on one task at a time and give it your full attention.

Another effective time management strategy is eliminating distractions; this can be challenging, especially in the age of technology, where we are constantly bombarded with notifications and alerts. To combat distractions, consider turning off notifications on your phone or computer when you need to focus on a task or find a quiet workplace where you can minimize distractions.

When managing your time, it is also essential to be mindful of your energy levels. Some people are more productive in the morning, while others may be more focused in the evening. Pay attention to your natural rhythms and try to schedule your most important tasks during your peak energy times.

One way to stay on track with your time management habits is to use a productivity tool, such as a planner or a to-do list app. These tools can help you organize tasks, set reminders, and track progress. First, however, finding a tool that works best for you and your specific needs is essential.

In addition to the strategies mentioned above, it is helpful to be flexible and willing to adjust your schedule as needed. Life is unpredictable, and things may require you to shift your priorities. Therefore, it is crucial to be able to adapt and make changes to your schedule as needed while still staying true to your overall goals.

Developing time management habits requires practice and discipline, but it can significantly impact your personal and professional life. By setting goals, creating a schedule, focusing on one task at a time, and using productivity tools, you can effectively manage your time and achieve your goals.

Chapter XIII. The Habit of Learning and Growth

Learning and growth are essential for personal and professional development; they allow us to acquire new skills, improve existing ones, and stay relevant in a constantly changing world. However, building the habit of learning and growth requires a proactive approach and a willingness to challenge ourselves and seek new opportunities continuously.

One way to foster the habit of learning and growth is to set specific goals; this can involve identifying a particular skill or area of knowledge you want to improve, and then creating a plan to achieve it; this might include taking a course or workshop, reading books or articles, or seeking out mentors or resources to guide you. Setting goals helps you stay focused and motivated, and it allows you to track your progress.

Another critical aspect of the habit of learning and growth is being open to new experiences and perspectives; this means being willing to try new things, even if they are outside your comfort zone. By stepping out of your comfort zone, you can expose yourself to new ideas and ways of thinking, which can broaden your horizons and help you grow.

One way to seek new experiences and perspectives is to seek diverse communities and resources; this might involve joining a club or organization, participating in online forums or groups, or networking with individuals from different backgrounds and industries. By engaging with diverse communities, you can learn from different perspectives and experiences and find new opportunities for growth.

Another effective strategy for fostering the habit of learning and growth is to be curious and ask questions; this means not being afraid to ask for clarification or seek out additional information when you don't understand something. By asking questions, you can deepen your understanding and gain new insights.

It is also vital to be proactive in seeking out opportunities for learning and growth; this might involve seeking out additional responsibilities at work, volunteering for a new project, or seeking out new challenges. By proactively seeking out opportunities, you can control your learning and growth and make the most of your time and resources.

Another aspect of the habit of learning and growth is the willingness to make mistakes and learn from them. Of course, no one is perfect, and making mistakes is a natural part of the learning process. However, by acknowledging your mistakes and using them as opportunities to learn and grow, you can build resilience and become more adaptable.

One way to build resilience and adaptability is to embrace a growth mindset. A growth mindset is a belief that skills and abilities can be developed and improved through effort and learning. By adopting a growth mindset, you can approach challenges and setbacks as opportunities for growth rather than setbacks.

In addition to the strategies mentioned above, it is also essential to prioritize learning and growth; this might involve setting aside dedicated time for learning or finding ways to integrate learning into your daily routine. Making learning and growth, a priority ensures that you continuously develop your skills and knowledge.

Developing the habit of learning and growth is an ongoing process that requires effort and discipline. However, by setting goals, seeking out new experiences and perspectives, being proactive and curious, and embracing a growth mindset, you can foster a lifelong habit of learning and growth that will benefit you personally and professionally.

Chapter XIV. The Habit of Self-Care

Self-care is taking care of one's physical, mental, and emotional well-being. It is an essential habit that is often overlooked in the hustle and bustle of everyday life. However, taking care of oneself is crucial for maintaining good health, reducing stress, and improving the overall quality of life.

One way to develop the habit of self-care is to prioritize self-care activities in your daily routine; this might involve setting aside dedicated time for self-care or finding ways to integrate self-care into your daily routine. For example, some everyday self-care activities include exercising, getting enough sleep, eating a healthy diet, and taking breaks from screens and technology. By prioritizing self-care activities, you can ensure that you take care of your physical and mental well-being daily.

Another critical aspect of the habit of self-care is paying attention to your needs and boundaries; this means being mindful of what you need to feel energized, balanced, and healthy and being willing to set boundaries to protect your well-being; this might involve saying no to commitments or activities that are not in alignment with your values or well-being or placing limits on your availability. By paying attention to your needs and setting boundaries, you can ensure that you are taking care of yourself and not overextending yourself.

One way to pay attention to your needs and set boundaries is to practice mindfulness. Mindfulness is the practice of being present and fully engaged in the present moment without judgment. By being mindful, you can become more aware of your thoughts, feelings, and needs, and you can make choices that align with your well-being.

Another critical aspect of the habit of self-care is self-compassion; this means being kind and understanding towards yourself, especially in times of struggle or failure. By practicing self-compassion, you can create a sense of inner support and resilience, which can help you navigate challenges and setbacks more effectively.

One way to practice self-compassion is to engage in self-care activities that nourish your mind, body, and soul; this might involve engaging in activities that bring you joy, such as hobbies, spending time in nature, or creative pursuits. It also consists of seeking out support from friends, family, or professionals when needed. You can build resilience and improve your well-being by nourishing yourself and seeking help.

In addition to the strategies mentioned above, it is also essential to be flexible and open to trying new self-care activities. What works for one person may not work for another, and it is crucial to find what works best for you. You can continuously improve your self-care habits by being open to trying new activities and approaches and seeing what works best for you.

Developing a self-care habit requires effort and discipline, but it is an essential habit that can significantly improve your physical, mental, and emotional well-being. By prioritizing self-care activities, paying attention to your needs and boundaries, practicing mindfulness and self-compassion, and being open to trying new activities, you can build a strong foundation of self-care that will benefit you in all areas of your life.

Chapter XV. The Habit of Communication and Relationships

Effective communication is a crucial skill that impacts all aspects of our lives, from personal relationships to professional success. It involves effectively conveying your thoughts, ideas, and feelings and listening actively and empathically to others. Building the habit of effective communication is not always easy, but it is essential for building and maintaining healthy relationships.

One way to develop the habit of effective communication is to be mindful of your communication style; this might involve examining your patterns of behavior, such as whether you tend to interrupt others, speak too quickly, or dominate conversations. By becoming more aware of your communication style, you can learn to adjust your behavior to be more effective in different situations.

Another critical aspect of the habit of effective communication is practicing active listening. Active listening involves entirely focusing on the person speaking and actively trying to understand their perspective. It involves paying attention not just to the words being spoken but also to nonverbal cues such as body language and facial expressions. You can build stronger relationships and improve your communication skills by practicing active listening.

One way to practice active listening is to paraphrase what the other person has said to show that you have heard and understood their perspective. It is also helpful to ask clarifying questions to show that you are interested and engaged in the conversation.

Another critical aspect of the habit of effective communication is to be assertive, rather than aggressive or passive. Assertiveness involves standing up for your own needs and beliefs while also being respectful of the needs and beliefs of others. Being assertive means communicating your needs and opinions effectively without causing conflict or resentment.

One way to practice assertiveness is to use "I" statements, rather than "you" statements. "I" statements focus on your feelings and needs rather than blaming or judging others. For example, rather than saying, "You never listen to me," you might say, "I feel hurt and frustrated when I feel like I am not being heard." Using "I" statements, you can express your feelings and needs more effectively and respectfully.

Another critical aspect of effective communication is being open and honest; this means being willing to share your thoughts and feelings, even if they may be difficult to express. By being open and honest, you can build trust and strengthen relationships.

One way to practice open and honest communication is to set aside dedicated time for conversations with loved ones or colleagues; this might involve scheduling regular check-ins or setting aside specific times to discuss important issues. Setting aside dedicated time for communication, you can ensure that you have the space to focus on meaningful conversations.

In addition to the strategies mentioned above, it is also essential to be flexible and open to feedback. Communication is a two-way process, and it is vital to be willing to listen to and consider the perspectives of others. You can continuously improve your communication skills and strengthen your relationships by being open to feedback.

Developing the habit of effective communication and relationships requires effort and discipline, but it is an essential habit that can greatly impact all aspects of your life. By being mindful of your own communication style, practicing active listening, and being assertive, open, honest, and open to feedback, you can build strong, healthy relationships and improve your communication skills.

Chapter XVI. The Habit of Creativity and Innovation

Creativity and innovation are essential skills that can be applied to a wide range of fields, from art and design to business and technology. They involve generating new ideas, thinking creatively, and finding novel solutions to problems. Building the habit of creativity and innovation requires a proactive approach and a willingness to embrace new perspectives and approaches.

One way to foster the habit of creativity and innovation is to cultivate a curious and open mindset; this means being open to new ideas and approaches and being willing to question assumptions and challenge the status quo. By embracing a curious and open attitude, you can create a more fertile ground for new ideas to emerge.

Another important aspect of the habit of creativity and innovation is to practice divergent thinking. Divergent thinking is the ability to generate a wide range of ideas and approaches to a problem rather than converging on a single solution. By practicing divergent thinking, you can expand your thinking and develop more creative solutions.

One way to practice divergent thinking is to engage in brainstorming sessions on your own or with a group. During a brainstorming session, it is essential to suspend judgment and generate as many ideas as possible, without evaluating their feasibility or quality. By developing a wide range of opinions, you can consider and refine them later to identify the most promising solutions.

Another critical aspect of the habit of creativity and innovation is to be willing to take risks and try new things; this might involve experimenting with new approaches, trying out new technologies, or pursuing new projects or ventures. By taking risks and trying new things, you can expose yourself to new experiences and ideas, which can spark creativity and innovation.

One way to take risks and try new things is to set aside dedicated time for experimentation and exploration; this might involve setting aside a specific time each week or month to try out new ideas or setting aside a particular budget for experimentation. You can create a more conducive environment for creativity and innovation by setting aside dedicated time and resources for exploration.

Another important aspect of the habit of creativity and innovation is to seek out diverse perspectives and resources; this might involve engaging with individuals or groups from different backgrounds and industries or seeking out resources such as books, articles, or workshops that can expose you to new ideas and approaches. By seeking diverse perspectives and resources, you can broaden your thinking and find new sources of inspiration.

In addition to the strategies mentioned above, it is essential to be resilient and adaptable. Innovation often involves experimentation and failure, and it is crucial to bounce back and learn from setbacks. By cultivating resilience and adaptability, you can become more resilient to challenges and more open to new ideas.

Developing the habit of creativity and innovation requires effort and discipline, but it is an essential habit that can significantly impact your personal and professional life. By cultivating a curious and open mindset, practicing divergent thinking, taking risks, trying new things, seeking out diverse perspectives and resources, and developing resilience and adaptability, you can foster a lifelong habit of creativity and innovation that will benefit you in all areas of your life.

Chapter XVII. The Habit of Leadership

Leadership is the ability to inspire and guide others toward a common goal. It involves the ability to communicate effectively, make decisions, and take responsibility for the actions of a group or organization. Building the leadership habit requires a proactive approach and a willingness to take on responsibilities and challenges.

One way to develop leadership habits is to set clear goals and communicate them effectively. This means identifying what you want to achieve, breaking down larger goals into smaller, more manageable tasks, and speaking them to others. You can create a shared sense of purpose and direction by setting clear goals and communicating them effectively.

Another critical aspect of the habit of leadership is to be proactive and take the initiative; this means being willing to identify problems or opportunities and taking action to address them. In addition, taking the initiative can demonstrate your commitment to the group or organization and inspire others to do the same.

One way to take the initiative is to identify areas where you can positively impact and take on additional responsibilities; this might involve volunteering for a new project or taking on different tasks within your current role. Taking on other duties can demonstrate your leadership skills and positively contribute to the group or organization.

Another important aspect of the leadership habit is to be a role model and lead by example; this means not only setting high standards for yourself but also consistently demonstrating behaviors that align with the group's or organization's values and goals. By being a role model, you can inspire others to follow your lead and contribute to the success of the group or organization.

One way to lead by example is to consistently demonstrate behaviors that align with the group's or organization's values and goals; this might involve setting aside dedicated time for professional development or actively seeking out opportunities to contribute to the group or organization. By consistently demonstrating behaviors that align with the values and goals of the group or organization, you can inspire others to do the same.

Another critical aspect of the habit of leadership is to be open and transparent in your communication and decision-making; this means being willing to share information, listening to perspectives, and being open to feedback and input. You can build trust and foster a collaborative and inclusive environment by being open and transparent.

One way to practice open and transparent communication is to set aside dedicated time for regular check-ins with team members or colleagues; this might involve scheduling regular meetings or one-on-one sessions to discuss progress and address any concerns or issues. You can create a more open and inclusive environment by setting aside dedicated time for regular check-ins.

In addition to the strategies mentioned above, it is learning and growing as a leader; this might involve seeking out opportunities for professional development, such as taking courses or workshops or seeking out mentors or resources to guide you. By continuously learning and growing as a leader, you can stay current and relevant and constantly improve your leadership skills.

Developing the habit of leadership requires effort and discipline, but it is an essential habit that can significantly impact your personal and professional life. By setting clear goals and communicating them effectively, taking the initiative, leading by example, being open and transparent, and continuously learning and growing, you can foster a lifelong habit of leadership that will benefit you in all areas of your life.

Chapter XVIII. The Habit of Finances and Productivity

Managing finances and being productive are essential skills for personal and professional success. They involve making wise financial decisions and using time and resources efficiently. Building the habit of managing finances and being productive requires a proactive approach and a willingness to prioritize and plan.

One way to develop the habit of managing finances is to create and stick to a budget; this means setting clear financial goals, tracking your income and expenses, and making conscious choices about allocating your money. By creating and sticking to a budget, you can make the most of your financial resources and reach your financial goals.

Another critical aspect of managing finances is being proactive in saving and investing; this means setting aside money for short-term and long-term goals and seeking out opportunities to grow your wealth. You can secure your financial future and prepare for unexpected expenses or opportunities by saving and investing.

One way to be proactive in saving and investing is to set aside dedicated time each month to review your finances and plan; this might involve setting aside money for savings and investments or seeking financial advisors or resources to guide you. By setting aside dedicated time and seeking guidance, you can make informed decisions about your finances and build a strong foundation for financial success.

Another critical aspect of managing finances is being mindful of spending; this means being aware of your financial habits and making conscious choices about allocating your money. By being mindful of spending, you can avoid overspending and make the most of your financial resources.

One way to be mindful of spending is to track your expenses and identify areas where you can cut back or make more informed choices; this might involve canceling unnecessary subscriptions or seeking discounts or deals. You can make the most of your financial resources by tracking your expenses and making more informed choices.

In addition to managing finances, being productive is also an important habit. Productivity involves using time and resources efficiently to achieve desired results. You can make the most of your time and resources and achieve your goals more effectively by being productive.

One way to be productive is to set clear goals and prioritize tasks. This means identifying what you want to achieve and breaking down larger goals into smaller, more manageable tasks. By setting clear goals and prioritizing tasks, you can focus on what is most important and make progress toward your goals.

Another key aspect of being productive is eliminating distractions and focusing on a single task; this might involve setting aside dedicated time for specific jobs or finding ways to minimize distractions, such as turning off notifications or finding a quiet workspace. By eliminating distractions and focusing on a single task at a time, you can increase your productivity and achieve your goals more efficiently.

In addition to the strategies mentioned above, it is also essential to be flexible and adaptable. Productivity often involves adapting to changing circumstances and priorities, and it is crucial to be able to adjust your approach as needed. You can become more productive and achieve your goals more effectively by cultivating flexibility and adaptability.

Chapter XIX. The Habit of Giving Back and Making a Difference

Giving back and making a difference involve taking actions that benefit others and contribute to the greater good. They involve a willingness to share resources, time, and skills to impact the world positively. Building the habit of giving back and making a difference requires a proactive approach and a sense of purpose and responsibility.

One way to develop the habit of giving back is to identify your passions and values and find ways to align them with your actions; this might involve volunteering your time or skills, supporting causes that align with your values or making charitable donations. By identifying your passions and values, you can find ways to make a meaningful and fulfilling difference.

Another critical aspect of giving back is being proactive in seeking opportunities to make a difference; this might involve seeking out organizations or causes that align with your passions and values or looking for ways to make a difference in your everyday life. By proactively seeking opportunities to make a difference, you can create a sense of purpose and fulfillment in your life.

One way to be proactive in seeking out opportunities to make a difference is to set aside dedicated time for volunteering or contributing to causes that align with your passions and values; this might involve setting aside a specific day each week or month to volunteer or setting aside a particular budget for charitable donations. You can make a more meaningful and lasting impact by dedicating time and resources to give back.

Another critical aspect of the habit of giving back is to be mindful of the impact of your actions; this means considering the long-term consequences of your choices and taking a responsible and sustainable approach to giving back. By being mindful of the impact of your actions, you can make a more positive and lasting difference in the world.

One way to be mindful of the impact of your actions is to research organizations and causes before supporting them, to ensure that they align with your values and have a positive effect. It is also essential to consider your choices' long-term consequences and look for ways to make a sustainable and lasting difference. By being mindful of the impact of your actions, you can make a more positive and lasting contribution to the world.

In addition to the strategies mentioned above, being humble and open to learning is essential. Giving back and making a difference often involves working with others and learning from diverse perspectives. Being humble and open to learning can expand your understanding and create a more meaningful and lasting difference in the world.

Developing the habit of giving back and making a difference requires effort and discipline, but it is an essential habit that can significantly impact your personal and professional life. By identifying your passions and values, being proactive in seeking out opportunities to make a difference, being mindful of the impact of your actions, and being humble and open to learning, you can foster a lifelong habit of giving back and making a difference that will benefit you and those around you.

Chapter XX. The Science Behind Habits

Habits are routine behaviors that are repeated frequently and automatically. Yet, they are a crucial aspect of our daily lives, as they allow us to perform tasks and make decisions without conscious thought. The science behind habits helps us understand how they form, how they can be changed, and how they impact our lives.

Habits are formed through habituation, which involves repeating behavior that becomes automatic over time. When we repeat a behavior, the neural pathways in our brain responsible for that behavior become more robust, making it easier to perform the behavior in the future.

One key aspect of the science behind habits is the role of the basal ganglia, a part of the brain that is responsible for habit formation. The basal ganglia stores information about habits and routines, allowing us to perform them automatically without conscious thought.

Another critical aspect of the science behind habits is the role of triggers or cues, which initiate a habit. Triggers can be external, such as a specific time or location, or internal, such as an emotion or thought. By recognizing the triggers that initiate our habits, we can better understand and modify them.

One way to modify a habit is to use the habit loop, which consists of a trigger, a behavior, and a reward. By identifying the trigger and reward of a habit, we can change the behavior by introducing a new habit in its place. For example, this might involve replacing an unhealthy habit, such as smoking, with a healthier habit, such as exercise.

Another critical aspect of the science behind habits is the role of willpower and self-control. Willpower is the ability to control our thoughts and actions, and it is a limited resource that can be depleted over time. Therefore, we can better manage our habits and make positive life changes by understanding the role of willpower and self-control in habit formation and modification.

In addition to the strategies mentioned above, it is essential to be patient and persistent when trying to change a habit. Habits take time to form and modify, and it is vital to be patient and persistent to see lasting change. By being patient and persistent, we can better manage and modify our habits to improve our lives.

The science behind habits helps us understand how they form, how they can be changed, and how they impact our lives. By understanding the role of the basal ganglia, triggers and cues, the habit loop, willpower and self-control, and the importance of patience and persistence, we can better manage and modify our habits to improve our lives.

Chapter XXI. The Habits of Successful People

Success is often achieved through the development of specific habits and behaviors. Successful people tend to have certain habits in common, such as setting goals, being proactive, and continuously learning and growing. Adopting these habits can increase our chances of success in our personal and professional lives.

One critical habit of successful people is setting goals. Successful people tend to have a clear vision of what they want to achieve, and they set specific, measurable, attainable, relevant, and time-bound (SMART, once again) goals to help them get there. By setting SMART goals, successful people can focus their efforts and make progress toward their desired outcomes.

Another essential habit of successful people is being proactive; this means taking the initiative, seeking out opportunities, and addressing challenges. By being proactive, successful people can create their luck and take control of their lives and careers.

One way to be proactive is to set aside time for planning and goal setting; this might involve creating a daily or weekly schedule that includes dedicated time for planning and reflection. By setting aside dedicated time for planning and goal setting, successful people can focus their efforts and progress toward their desired outcomes.

Another critical habit of successful people is continuously learning and growing; this means being open to new ideas, seeking new experiences and learning opportunities, and being willing to challenge themselves and their assumptions. By continuously learning and growing, successful people are able to stay current and relevant, and they are able to adapt and thrive in a constantly changing world.

One way to continuously learn and grow is to set aside dedicated time for professional development and learning; this might involve taking courses or workshops, reading books or articles, or seeking mentors or coaches to guide you. By setting aside dedicated time for learning and professional development, successful people can stay current and relevant and continuously improve their skills and knowledge.

Another essential habit of successful people is being resilient and adaptable; this means being able to bounce back from setbacks and challenges and adapt and thrive in changing circumstances. By being resilient and flexible, successful people can overcome obstacles and continue making progress toward their goals.

One way to cultivate resilience and adaptability is to practice self-care and seek support when needed; this might involve engaging in activities that nourish your mind and soul, such as hobbies, creative pursuits, camping, hiking or outdoor activities. It also consists of seeking out support from friends, family, or professionals when needed. By practicing self-care and seeking help, successful people can build resilience and adaptability.

In addition to the habits mentioned above, successful people also tend to have strong communication and relationship skills. They can effectively communicate their ideas and thoughts and build and maintain strong relationships with others. Successful people can build trust and foster collaboration and teamwork by cultivating strong communication and relationship skills.

Developing the habits of successful people requires effort and discipline, but it is an essential step toward achieving success in all areas of life. By setting goals, being proactive, continuously learning and growing, being resilient and adaptable, and cultivating strong communication and relationship skills, we can increase our chances of success and achieve our desired outcomes.

Chapter XXII. The Connection Between Habits and Happiness

Habits play a significant role in our overall well-being and happiness. They can either support or hinder our happiness, depending on whether they are positive or negative habits. Therefore, we can increase our overall happiness and well-being by cultivating positive habits and reducing negative habits.

One fundamental connection between habits and happiness is the role of mindfulness. As we stated before, mindfulness involves paying attention to the present moment with non-judgmental awareness, and it has been shown to increase overall well-being and happiness. Therefore, cultivating mindfulness through meditation or mindful breathing can improve our overall happiness and well-being.

Another meaningful connection between habits and happiness is the role of gratitude. Gratitude involves actively focusing on the positive aspects of our lives, and it has been shown to increase overall well-being and happiness. We can improve our overall happiness and well-being by cultivating gratitude through habits such as keeping a journal or expressing gratitude to others.

One way to cultivate gratitude is to set aside dedicated time each day to focus on the positive aspects of our lives. For example, this might involve writing down a list of things we are grateful for or sharing them with others. We can increase our overall happiness and well-being by setting aside dedicated time to focus on gratitude.

Another critical connection between habits and happiness is the role of positive social relations. Social solid links have been shown to increase overall well-being and happiness, and building and maintaining positive relationships is an important habit that can contribute to overall happiness.

One way to cultivate positive social connections is to set aside dedicated time for socializing and building relationships; this might involve making time for regular coffee dates, dinner parties, or joining a club or organization that aligns with your interests. We can increase our overall happiness and well-being by setting aside dedicated time for socializing and building relationships.

In addition to the habits mentioned above, focusing on overall well-being and self-care is crucial; this involves taking care of physical and mental health and making choices that support overall well-being. By focusing on overall well-being and self-care, we can increase our overall happiness and well-being.

One way to focus on overall well-being and self-care is to set aside dedicated time for activities that nourish the mind and body, such as exercise, meditation, or hobbies. It is also essential to pay attention to nutrition and seek preventive care to maintain physical health. By focusing on overall well-being and self-care, we can increase our overall happiness and well-being.

The connection between habits and happiness is significant, and cultivating positive habits can significantly increase our overall happiness and well-being. By cultivating mindfulness, gratitude, positive social relationships, and overall well-being and self-care, we can improve our overall happiness and well-being.

Chapter XXIII. Three Real-life Individuals Who Used the Compound Effect of Habits

In this last chapter, we will explore the lives of three real-life individuals who have successfully used the power of the compound effect of habits to transform their lives. These individuals faced unique challenges and started from different points in their journey. Still, they all managed to overcome obstacles and achieve their goals through the consistent application of good habits.

J.K. Rowling

J.K. Rowling is best known as the author of the Harry Potter series, one of the most successful book and film franchises in history. However, before she became a globally renowned author, Rowling was a struggling single mother living on welfare in Edinburgh, Scotland.

In the mid-1990s, Rowling began writing the first Harry Potter book while working as a researcher and bilingual secretary for the Manchester Chamber of Commerce. She faced numerous challenges while writing the book, including a lack of time and money and the need to care for her young daughter. Despite these challenges, Rowling persevered and eventually finished the book.

One of the critical habits that helped Rowling overcome these challenges was her commitment to writing every day, no matter what. In an interview with Oprah Winfrey, Rowling revealed that she wrote the first Harry Potter book while her daughter was napping and made a point of writing at least 1000 words daily. This daily writing habit allowed Rowling to make steady progress on her book and eventually complete it.

In addition to her daily writing habit, Rowling also developed a habit of seeking out opportunities to learn and improve her craft. For example, she took a creative writing course at the University of Edinburgh, and she actively sought out feedback on her work from friends and mentors. These habits helped Rowling develop her writing skills and eventually led to the publication of the Harry Potter series.

Today, J.K. Rowling is widely recognized as one of the most successful authors of all time, and her story inspires anyone who wants to turn their passion into a successful career.

Tim Ferriss

Tim Ferriss is an entrepreneur, investor, and author who has become well-known for his work on personal development and productivity. In his best-selling book, "The 4-Hour Work Week," Ferriss shares his experiences and insights on streamlining and optimizing one's life to achieve more with less time and effort.

Ferriss's journey to success began when he was a salesperson for a data storage company. Despite his initial success in sales, Ferriss felt unfulfilled and constantly sought ways to optimize his work and personal life. As a result, he began experimenting with different habits and strategies, such as using technology to automate tasks, outsourcing work to freelancers, and using mindfulness and meditation to improve his focus and productivity.

One of the critical habits that Ferriss credits with helping him achieve success is his commitment to continuous learning and improvement. Ferriss is an avid reader and constantly seeks new ideas and problem-solving approaches. He also habitually breaks down complex tasks into smaller, more manageable chunks and focuses on one job at a time.

In addition to his commitment to learning and focus, Ferriss has a habit of setting clear and specific goals for himself and then developing a plan to achieve those goals. This habit has helped Ferriss focus his efforts and steady progress toward his objectives.

Ferriss's continuous learning, focus, and goal-setting habits have helped him achieve success in many areas, including entrepreneurship, investing, and writing. His book, "The 4-Hour Work Week," has become a best-seller, and he has built a large following of devoted fans and followers inspired by his ideas and strategies for achieving success.

Tony Robbins

Tony Robbins is a well-known motivational speaker, author, and personal development coach who has helped millions of people to transform their lives and achieve their goals. Robbins's journey to success began in the early 1980s when he worked as a janitor and struggled to make ends meet.

Despite his difficult circumstances, Robbins was determined to improve his life and achieve success. He began reading books on personal development and seeking mentors who could help him learn and grow. Through his efforts and the guidance of others, Robbins developed several habits that allowed him to transform his life.

One of the critical habits contributing to Robbins's success is his commitment to personal growth and self-improvement. Robbins has a habit of setting clear and specific goals for himself and then developing a plan to achieve those goals. He also has a habit of seeking opportunities to learn and grow through formal education and personal experiences.

In addition to his commitment to personal growth, Robbins also has a habit of maintaining a positive attitude and focusing on solutions rather than problems. This habit has helped him to overcome challenges and setbacks and to stay motivated and focused on his goals.

Through his consistent application of good habits, Tony Robbins has achieved a level of success that is unparalleled in his field. He has helped millions of people to transform their lives and achieve their goals, and his work has inspired countless others to pursue their dreams and aspirations.

The stories of J.K. Rowling, Tim Ferriss, and Tony Robbins demonstrate the power of the compound effect of habits to transform a person's life. These individuals faced unique challenges and started from different points in their journey. Still, they all managed to overcome obstacles and achieve their goals through the consistent application of good habits.

Whether you seek to improve your career, relationships, or overall quality of life, habits' compound effect can help you progress toward your goals. By developing good habits and consistently applying them over time, you can create positive changes in your life that will have a lasting impact.

Conclusion

In conclusion, lasting building habits are essential to personal and professional growth. Habits shape our daily lives and influence our overall well-being and success. By understanding the science behind habits and adopting the habits of successful people, we can increase our chances of achieving our goals and leading fulfilling lives.

Cultivating positive habits and reducing negative patterns is an ongoing process that requires effort and discipline. It involves being proactive and setting clear goals, continuously learning, and growing, being resilient and adaptable, and focusing on overall well-being and self-care. We can create a foundation for lasting personal and professional growth by cultivating these habits.

In addition to the habits mentioned above, it is also essential to be mindful of our actions impact, give back, and make a difference in the world. By being mindful of the effects of our actions and giving back to others, we can create a sense of purpose and fulfillment that adds to our overall happiness and well-being.

Developing lasting habits is not a one-time event but a lifelong process requiring commitment and dedication. It needs us to be proactive, to continuously learn and grow, and to be patient and persistent in our efforts. By embracing this process and cultivating lasting habits, we can achieve personal and professional growth and lead fulfilling and successful lives.